THE JOURNEY OF THE RED HORSE

THE JOURNEY OF THE RED HORSE

HORSE AND STAG PAINTINGS

VALENTINA DUBASKY

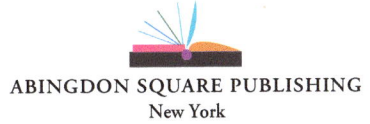

ABINGDON SQUARE PUBLISHING
New York

**The Journey of the Red Horse:
Horse and Stag Paintings**
published by
Abingdon Square Publishing
463 West Street, Suite G122
New York, NY 10014
USA
www.abingdonsquarepublishing.com
Book design: Abingdon Square Publishing

For information contact:
Valentina DuBasky
www.valentinadubasky.com

ISBN: 978-0-9830762-7-8
Library of Congress Control Number: 2016939872

Printed in the United States of America

Cover: *Vermilion Horse in Pink Field,* oil on canvas, 72 x 60 inches, 2016

TABLE OF CONTENTS

ARTIST'S STATEMENT

The correspondences between ancient art and the contemporary imagination is an abiding theme in my paintings. In the large paintings, works on paper and prints, I juxtapose totemic animals with petroglyphs and plants that appear and fade within layers of paint to suggest a natural ecosystem in which all life is interdependent. While some of the paintings depict groups of creatures, other paintings often include a single-image of a horse, stag or bison that is pitched on the edge of abstraction and can be read as animal, abstraction, landscape or still life. These paintings, sometimes described as magical realist, are inspired by my travels along the Silk Route in China, India, Central Asia and Southeast Asia, where I researched Buddhist cave paintings and ancient art to prepare for my own modern-day, cave-wall paintings.

THE LARGE PAINTINGS

The inspiration for the new large paintings on exhibit at Carter Burden Gallery in New York reflect several overlapping paths of inspiration: totemic animal images, the pre-perspectival surfaces of cave art, the seduction of drawings discovered in ancient manuscripts, and the process of making a painting with collage-like forms that bind content to form. Each of these streams of inquiry informs the visceral experience of specific landscapes and the creatures that inhabit those places.

The Journey of the Red Horse paintings reflects direct experiences with specific places, both real and imagined. They were painted in response to the ancient art and physical landscapes of the Silk Route in South Asia, Central Asia and Southeast Asia. I had started painting groupings of horses, stags and birds after traveling on the Silk Route in Western China where I had gone to research Buddhist Cave paintings in preparation for my own modern-day, cave-wall paintings. Later, I visited Buddhist cave sites in India and still later, traveled north toward the Himalayas. The ancient animals in the art of the Silk Route and divergent mountain routes entered my imagination, where they leap, gallop and turn, and sometimes observe the activities of humans.

Several of the large paintings were inspired by a recent visit to the Seima Protection Forest in Cambodia, the last remaining tract of wilderness in Southeast Asia. Later in my studio, it was wonderful to imagine an abundance of animal life in the forest as I worked on the paintings. Created with brushes and palette knife, the animals appear and fade within the layers of paint, as if carved and drawn onto a cave wall, the red horse standing at the bottom. One of these, Indian River Horse is a painting about a group of animals along an imaginary river journey and the moment of flight that sets a wilderness in sudden motion. The red spotted horse and companion amber bird are set in a field of pinks, oranges and yellows with imaginary plants and branches. The paintings are about a journey that begins in a field of color.

HORSE AND STAG PAINTINGS

Here is a story about how the Horse and Stag Paintings began. One night in Vermont, I took a walk. By the light of the moon, I saw several large white cows and they appeared to me to be perfect rectangles. This opened the way to painting image on the edge of abstraction; of exploring figurative expressionism.

The horse paintings are made with thick, impasto, oil paint and calligraphic gesture and line. In Spotted Horse in Claret Field, I combined impasto paint and calligraphic brushwork to express both the horse and background field in reds, umbers and blacks. In other paintings, the rectangle is divided. Amber Horse is inspired by the Amber Route, an ancient trade route that linked northern Europe with ancient Rome. Amber, a resin, collects and reflects light. This function of transforming the impression of light through the process of hardening is similar in effect to the wax and drying oil I use with the oil paint.

The horse paintings offer a dual reading in which the painting can be seen as abstracted horse or a still life table. The animal's rectangular body becomes a tabletop that often contains a mark that can be read either as a vessel or as a mark on the horse's flank. We have two readings: wild animal and human's table, two poles of the untamed and the domesticated.

It is interesting to think about how people decorate their horses. Horses are outfitted in decorative tack, tassels and precious metals that are functional, ceremonial or shamanic. There are many examples in Indian manuscript paintings and ancient nomadic art in which the stamp of human domestication of horses exists in tandem with the stamp of a horses hoof. Red Horse with Bells depicts the impact of the human hand as creator of the decoration embellishing the horse expressed through my brush marks and mark-making. The act of decorating a horse speaks to the intertwined destiny of horses with humankind.

In this collection of modern-day cave-wall paintings, I explore the bond between humans and depicted animals that live within the human psyche. The paintings are my response to the animal within.

The exhibition also includes two stag paintings. Stags and deer in cave paintings and ancient art have often been a source of inspiration for my work. Ancient stags appear in the cave paintings of Lascaux in France and Altamira in Spain; they are seen in Buddhist cave paintings along the ancient Silk Route in China; and are incised into sacred Deer Stones in wild Mongolia depicting leaping stags with spiraling antlers. In the stag paintings, I follow the link of the stag from its source in ancient art along a continuum that stretches from cave paintings to figurative expressionism.

Valentina DuBasky
New York, 2016

LARGE PAINTINGS

RED HORSE AND CRANE
Oil on canvas, 72 x 60 inches, 2016

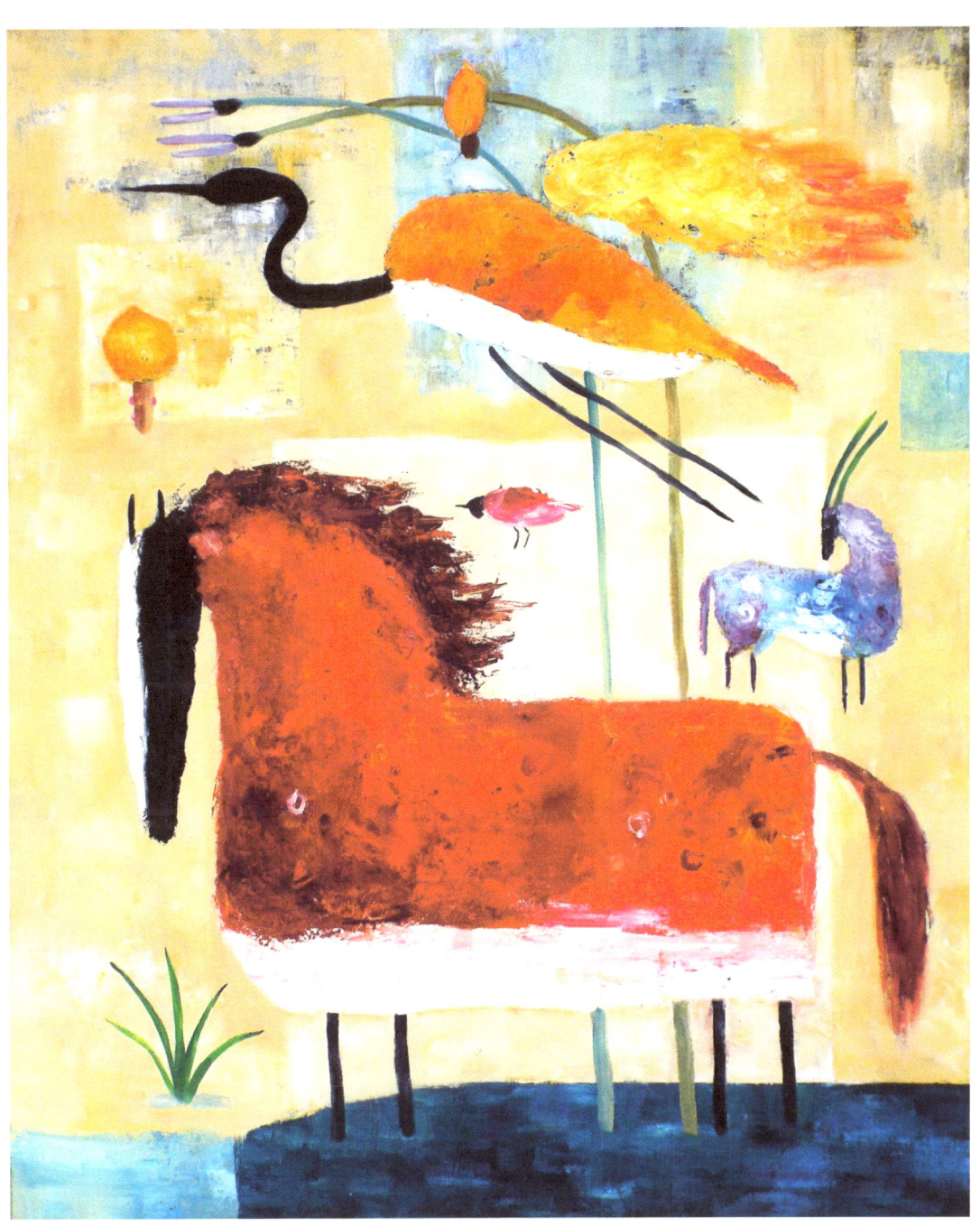

HIMALAYAN HORSE AND GAZELLE
Oil on canvas, 72 x 60 inches, 2016

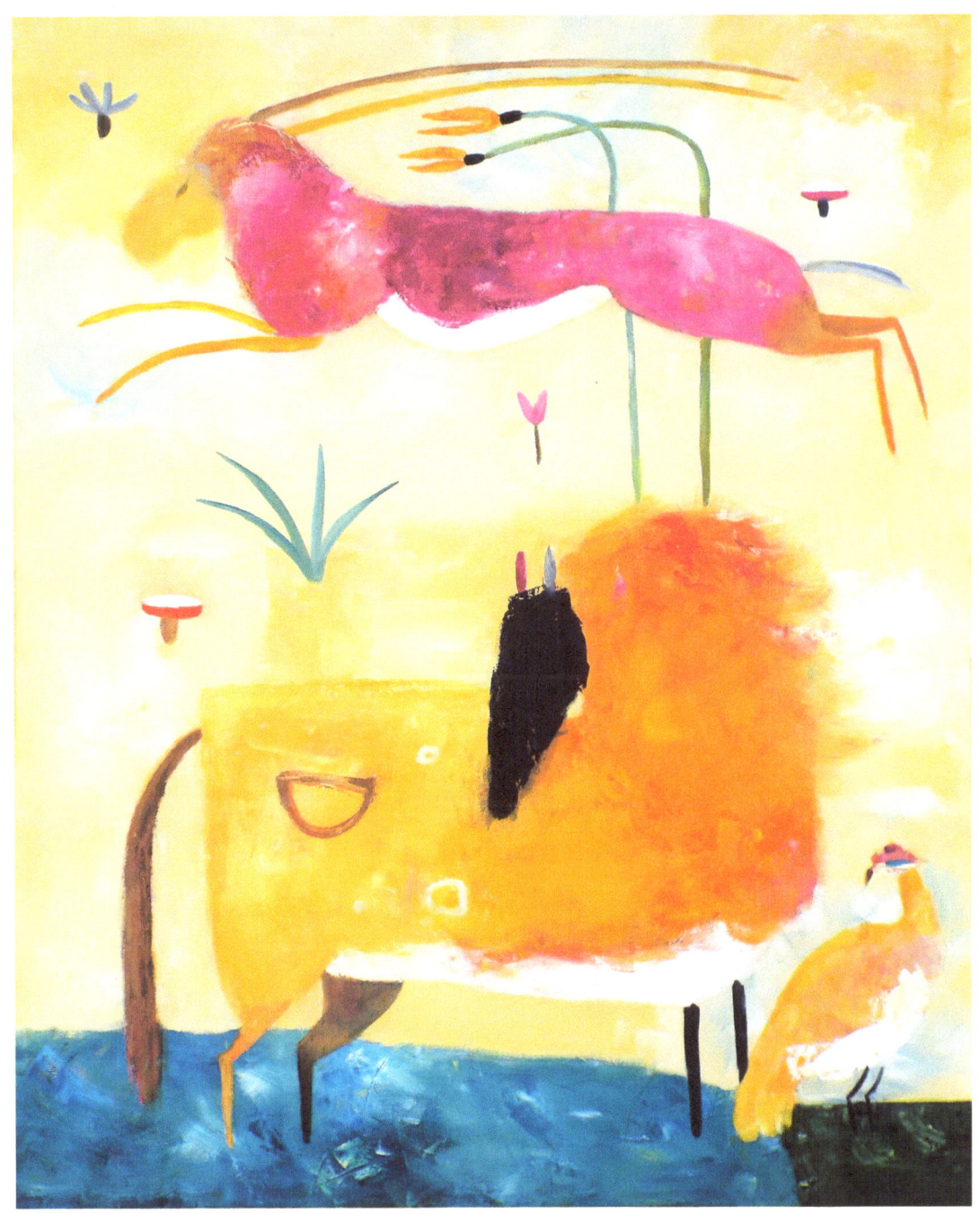

THE PROTECTED FOREST
Oil on canvas, 72 x 66 inches, 2016

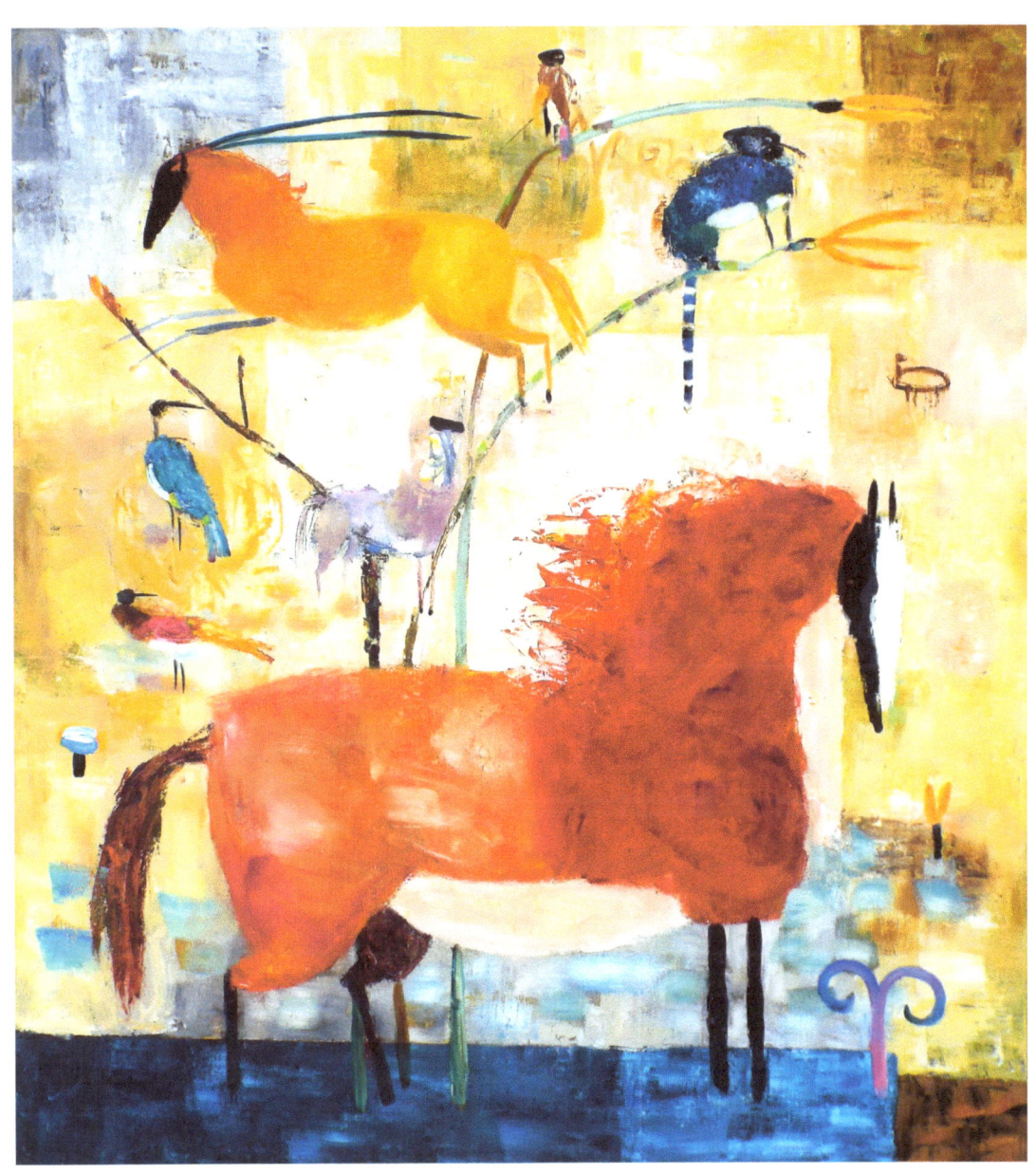

VERMILION HORSE IN PINK FIELD
Oil on canvas, 72 x 60 inches, 2016

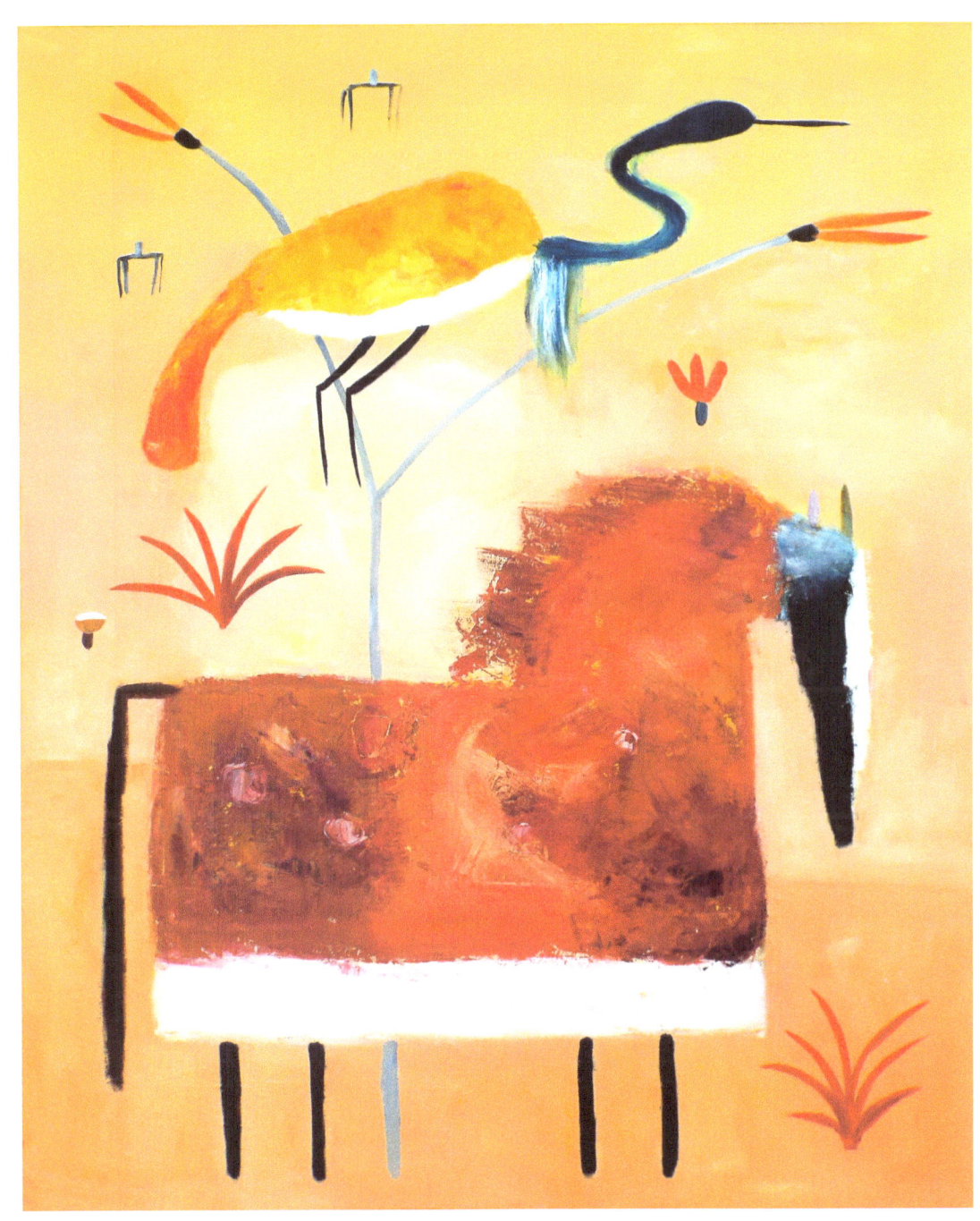

13

INDIAN RIVER HORSE
Oil on canvas, 72 x 66 inches, 2016

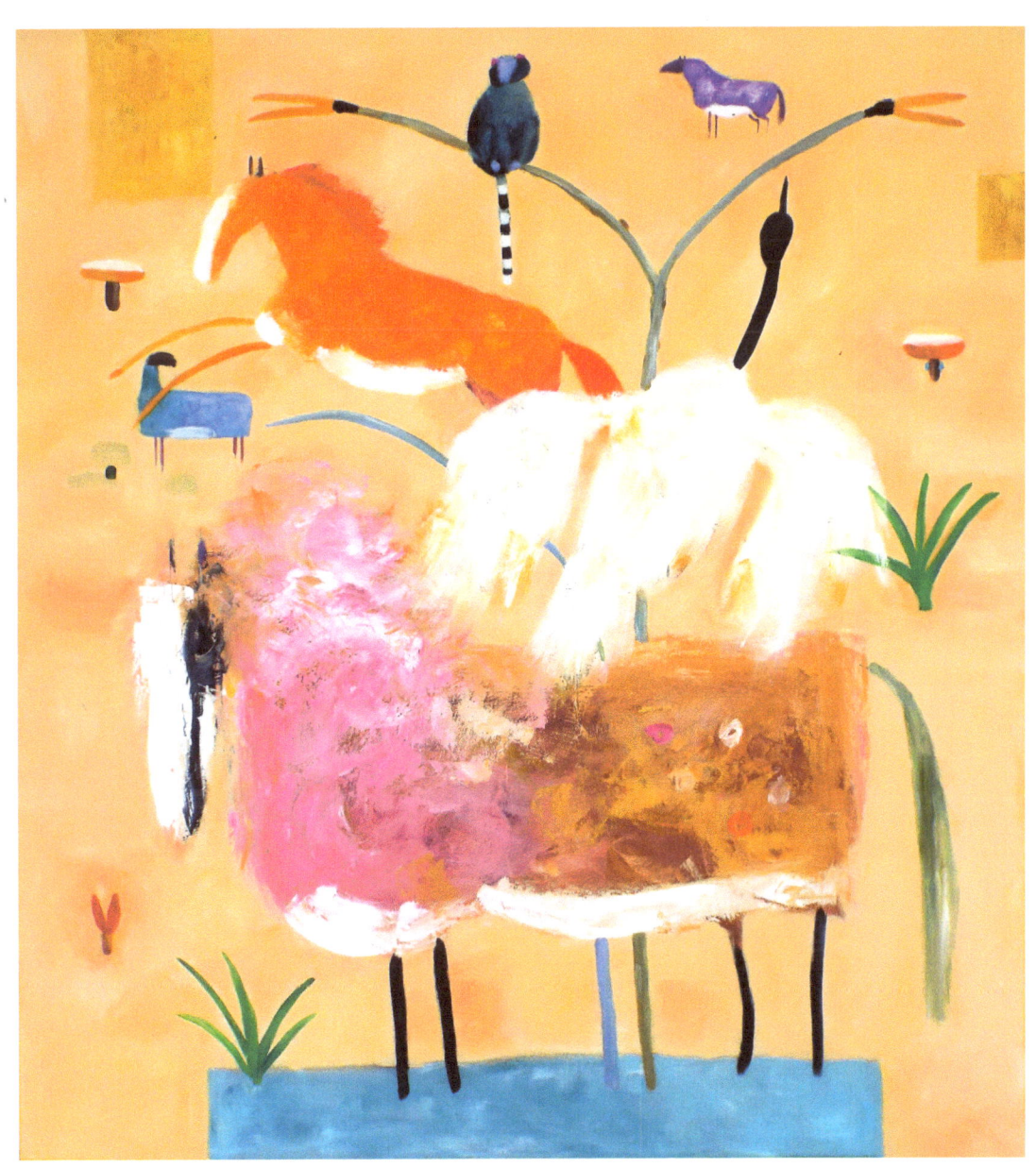

HORSE AND STAG
PAINTINGS

GRAY STAG IN RUSSET FIELD
Oil on canvas, 31 x 26 inches, 2012

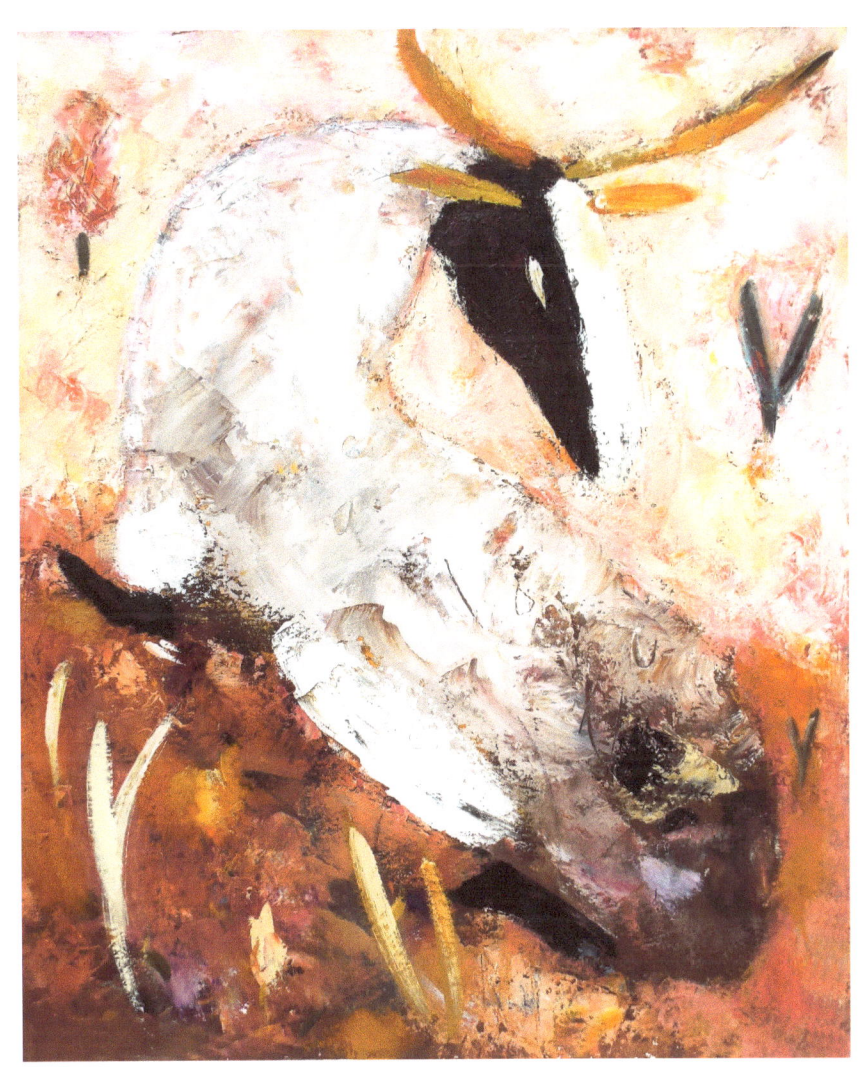

CLARET STAG IN RUSSET FIELD
Oil on canvas, 31 x 26 inches, 2012

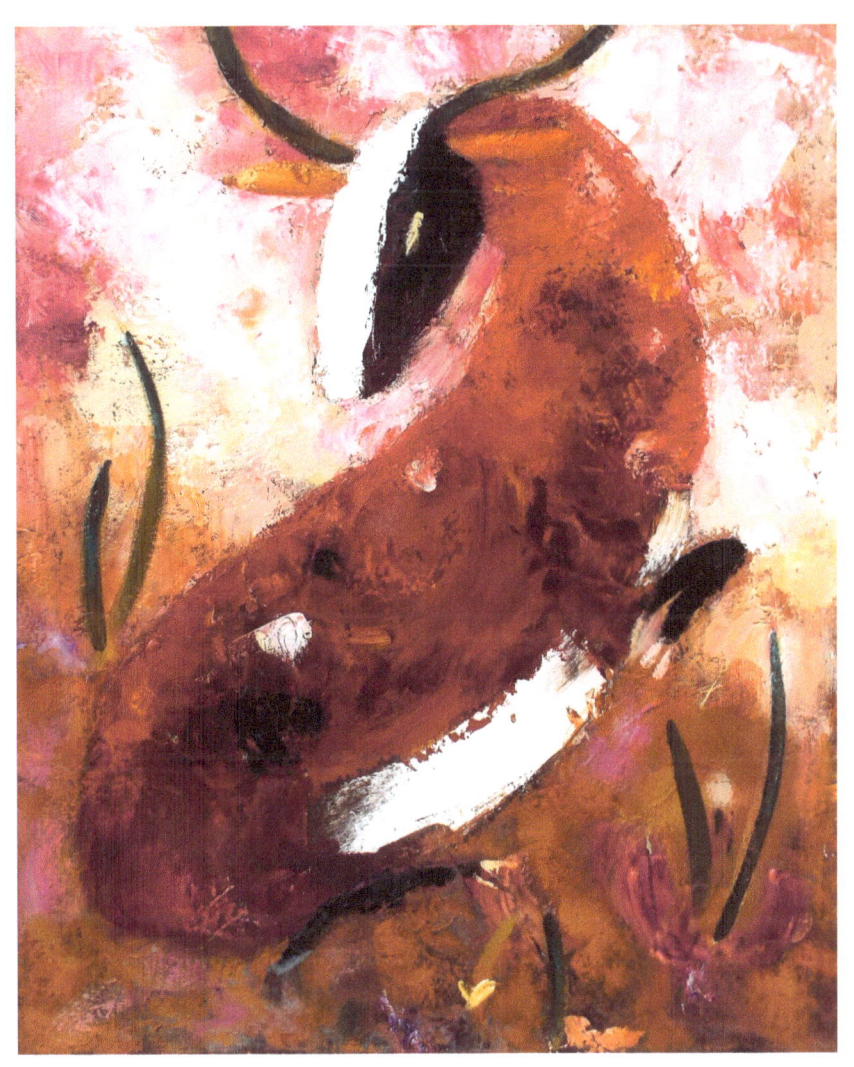

RED HORSE WITH BELLS
Oil on canvas, 22 x 30 inches, 2016

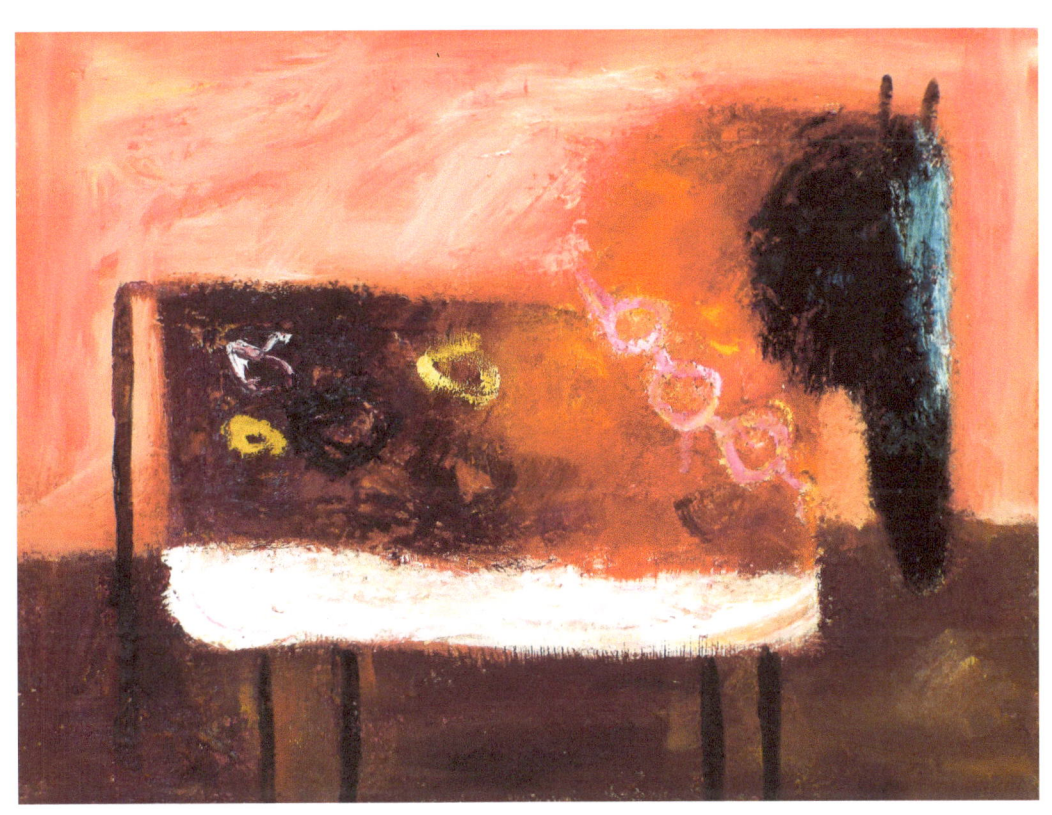

SIENNA HORSE WITH BELLS
Oil on paper, 22 x 30 inches, 2016

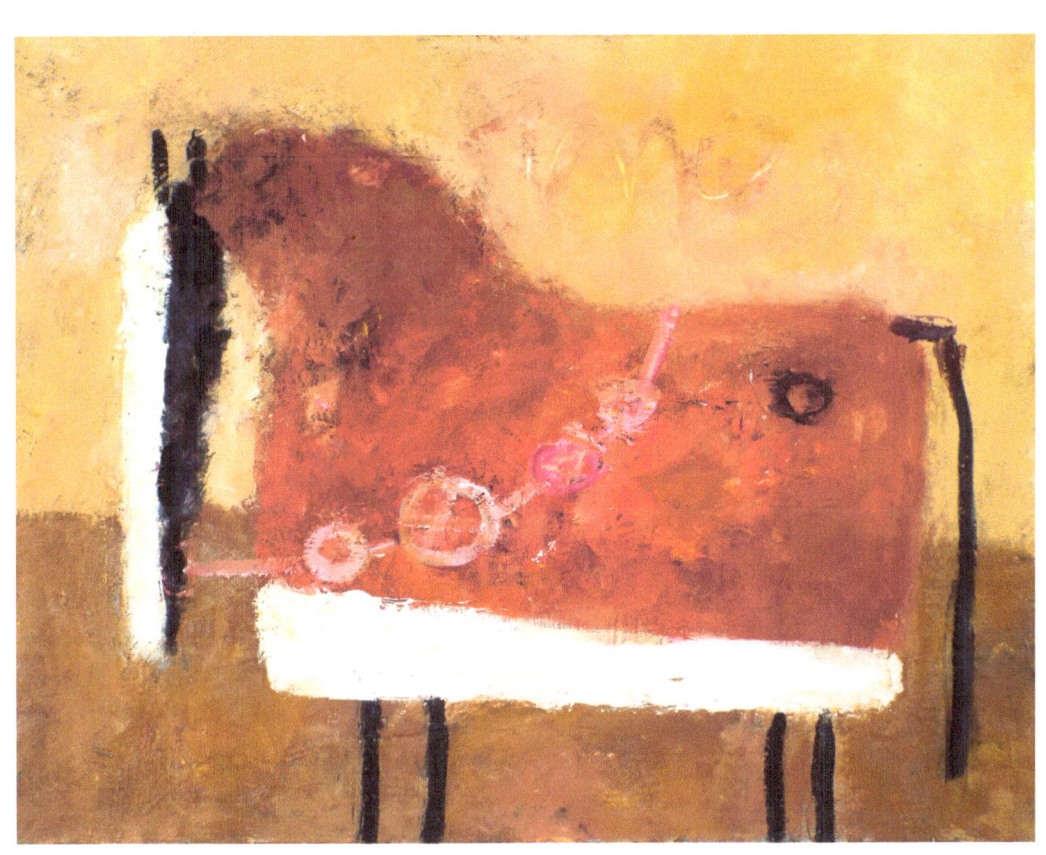

25

RED SPLIT HORSE
Oil on canvas, 22 x 30 inches, 2016

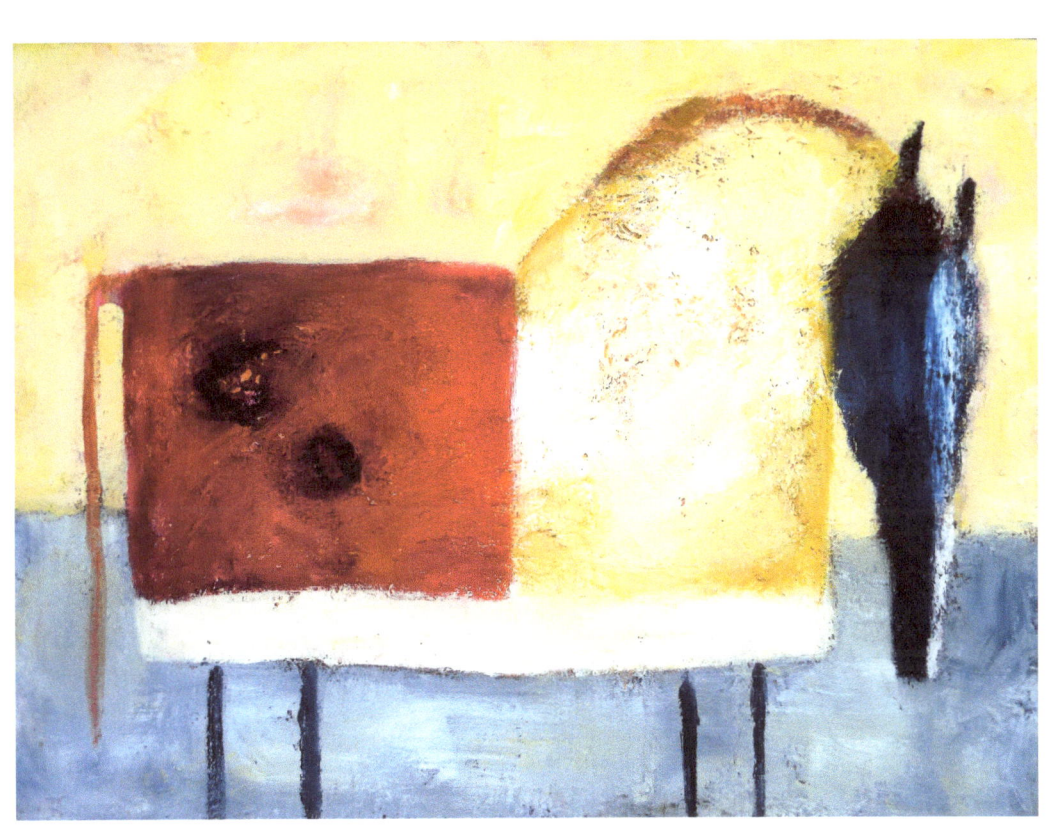

SPOTTED HORSE IN CLARET FIELD
Oil on canvas, 22 x 30 inches, 2016

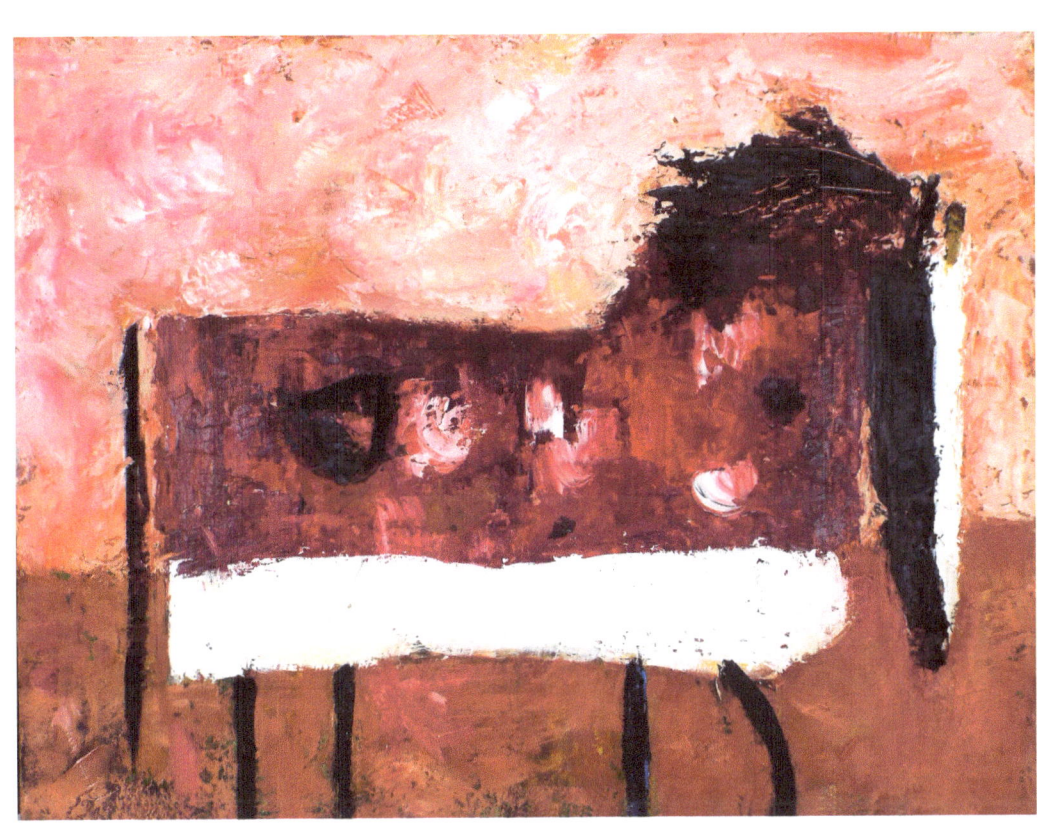

AMBER HORSE
Oil on canvas, 22 x 30 inches, 2013

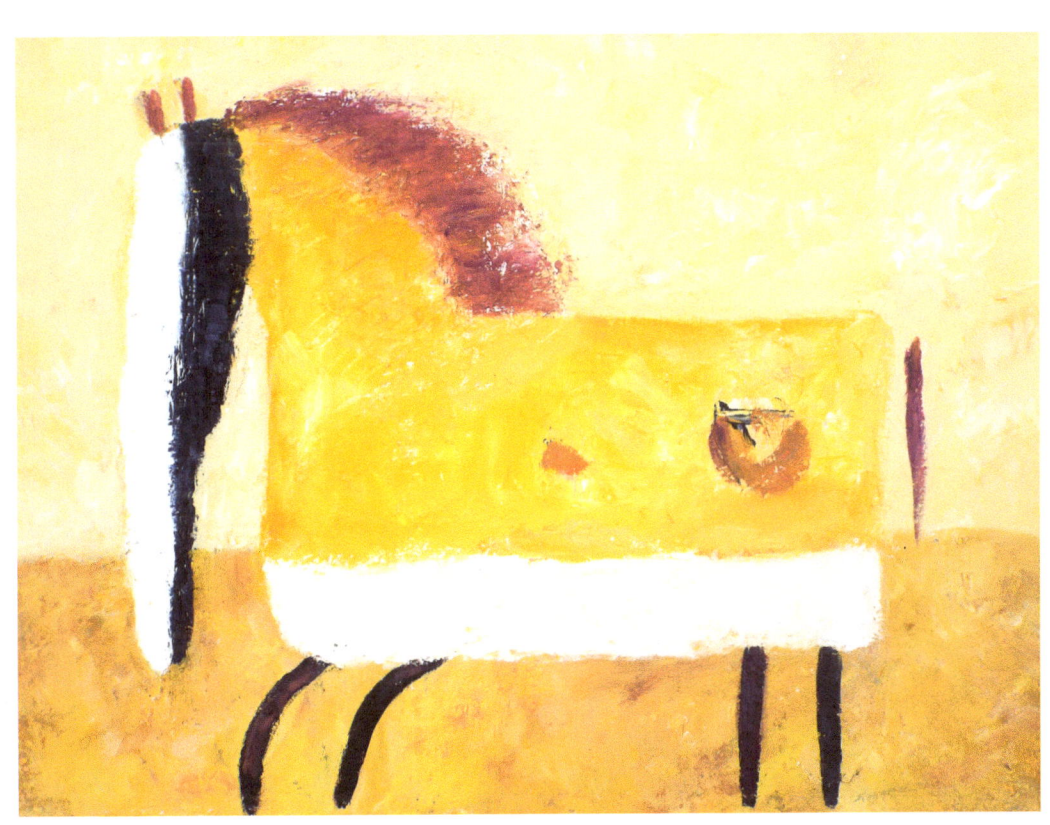

RED AND WHITE SPOTTED HORSE
Oil on canvas, 22 x 30 inches, 2016

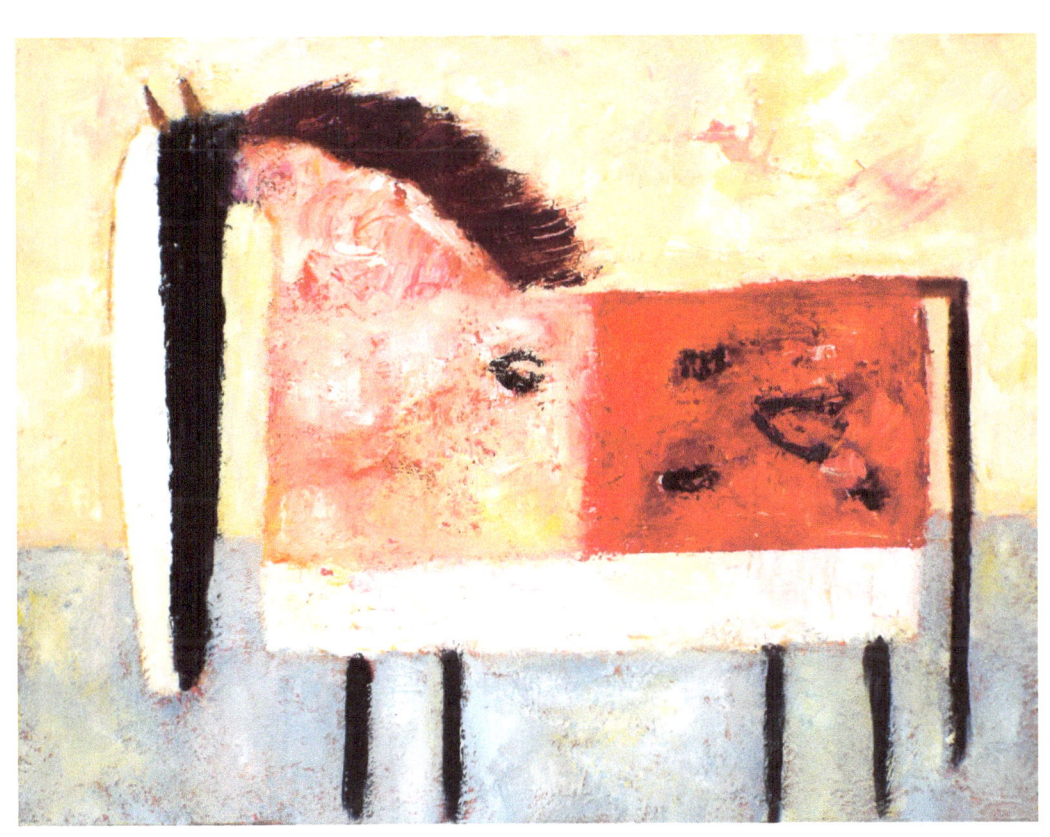

RESUME

ONE-PERSON EXHIBITIONS

2008   "Mongolian Horses and Siberian Tigers", Cheryl Pelavin Fine Arts, New York, NY
"Cambodian Flower Archaeology Monotypes", Cheryl Pelavin Fine Arts, New York, NY

2006   "Review: Cranes, Herons and Waterbirds", Cheryl Pelavin Fine Arts, New York, NY
"Preview: Rainforests, Cloudforests and Pine", Cheryl Pelavin Fine Arts, New York, NY
"Paintings", College of the Marshall Islands, Majuro, Republic of the Marshall Islands

2005   "The Crane Series", Ogilvie-Pertl Gallery, Chicago, IL
"Riverbirds & Rainforests", The National Academies of Sciences, Washington, DC
"Materia Medica", The Creative Center, New York, NY

2004   "The Crane & Heron Series", Cheryl Pelavin Fine Arts, New York, NY
"Paintings by Valentina DuBasky", Friesen Fine Arts, Sun Valley, ID
"Atlantic Flyway Project", Teaneck Creek Conservancy, Teaneck, NJ

2002   "New Paintings", Hodges Taylor Gallery, Charlotte, NC
"New Paintings", Friesen Fine Arts, Sun Valley, ID

2001   "New Paintings", Silpakorn University Art Center Gallery, Bangkok, Thailand
"Orchids and Fossils: New Landscape Paintings", Cheryl Pelavin Fine Arts, New York, NY

2000   "Ancient Futures: New Paintings & Monoprints", Cheryl Pelavin Fine Arts, New York, NY
"Representation Debut," Friesen Fine Arts, Seattle, WA
"Orchids on the Way to the Temple", Galerie Timothy Tew, Atlanta, GA
"Through Bending Trees", Friesen Fine Arts, Sun Valley, ID

1998   "Memory and Light: New Paintings", Cheryl Pelavin Fine Arts, New York, NY
"Materia Medica: New Monoprints", Cheryl Pelavin Fine Arts, New York, NY

1997   "Paintings", Hodges Taylor Gallery, Charlotte, NC
"Landscape, Archaeology & Memory, Paintings, Sculpture & Monoprints 1985-97",
     University of North Carolina Gallery, Asheville, NC

1995   "Painting Retrospective", Rena Haveson Gallery, Pittsburgh, PA
"Photographs", Gallery f32, Asheville, NC

1991   "New Paintings", Ruth Siegel Gallery, New York, NY

1990   "New Paintings", Ruth Siegel Gallery, New York, NY

1987   "Bronze Sculpture from the Caravan Series", Empire Bronze Art Gallery, LIC, NY

1986   "Paintings on Paper", Oscarsson-Siegeltuch Gallery, New York, NY
"Paintings & Monotypes", Hodges Banks Gallery, Seattle, WA

1985   "Recent Paintings", van Straaten Gallery, Chicago, IL
"Recent Paintings", Oscarsson Hood Gallery, New York, NY
"Paintings from the Stag Series", Gloria Luria Gallery, Miami, FL
"Monotypes", Jay Gallery, New York, NY

1984   "Recent Paintings", Susan Montazenos Gallery, Philadelphia, PA

1983   "Paintings from the Stag Series", Oscarsson Hood Gallery, New York, NY
"Recent Paintings", Robert L. Kidd Gallery, Detroit, MI

1981   "Paintings on Paper", Oscarsson Hood Gallery, New York, NY

1980   "Paintings", Semaphore Gallery, New York, NY

SELECTED GROUP EXHIBITIONS

2016   "Journeys", Two-person show, Carter Burden Gallery, New York, NY

2015   "Small Works", Carter Burden Gallery, New York, NY
       "True Monotypes", International Print Center New York,
          Curated by Janice Oresman, New York, NY
       "Group Exhibition", McElwain Fine Arts, St Louis, MO

2014   "Shifting Ecologies", The Painting Center, New York, NY
       "Tandem Press Monoprints", Expo Chicago, IL
       "Tandem Press Monoprints", IFPDA Print Fair, New York Armory, New York, NY
       "Tandem Press Monoprints", NYINK Art Fair, Miami Beach, FL

2013   "Tandem Press Monoprints", IFPDA Print Fair, New York Armory, New York, NY
       "Tandem Press Monoprints", NYINK Art Fair, Miami Beach, FL

2010   "Spring Prints", Cheryl Pelavin Fine Arts, New York, NY

2009   "Paintings", Friesen Fine Arts, Seattle, WA
       "Streetscapes", Landscapes, Still Lives, Jan Larsen Art, New York, NY
       "Art and Democracy", Gallery H, New York, NY

2008   "Friends", Cheryl Pelavin Fine Arts, New York, NY
       "From Different Horizons of Rock Shelter", Pang Mapha Archaeological Site, Thailand
       "From Different Horizons of Rock Shelter", National Gallery of Art, Bangkok, Thailand
       "Print Show", Cheryl Pelavin Fine Arts, New York, NY

2007   "25 Years of Printmaking at Cheryl Pelavin Fine Arts", Cheryl Pelavin Fine Arts, New York, NY

2006   "Alignment", Friesen Fine Art, Seattle, WA
       "Oil & Wax", Robert Roman Galleries, Scottsdale, AZ
       "Group Show", Ogilvie-Pertl Gallery, Chicago, IL
       "Art Scottsdale", Ogilvie-Pertl Gallery & Larsen Gallery, Scottsdale, AZ
       "Traveling Exhibition: Agent Orange: Consequence of War, a Call to Conscience",
          Marlboro College Gallery, Vermont; Brandeis University Gallery, Boston;
          George Washington University Gallery, Washington, DC

2005   "Oil & Wax: Chapter & Verse", Siano Gallery, Philadelphia, PA

2004   "Two Artists", Ogilvie-Pertl Gallery, Chicago, IL
       "The New Realism", Robert L. Kidd Gallery, Detroit, MI
       "Two Artists: Reflections of Cambodia", The Puffin Foundation, Teaneck, NJ
       "Returning the Brownfields of Teaneck Creek", Teaneck Creek Conservancy, Teaneck, NJ
       "Toxic Landscape", Long Beach Island Foundation of the Arts & Sciences, Love Ladies, NJ
       "Lower Manhattan Cultural Council Benefit", DKNY, New York, NY
       "Dealer's Choice", Robert L. Kidd Gallery, Detroit, MI

2003   "Flora and Fauna: Manifestations", Cheryl Pelavin Fine Arts, New York, NY
       "American Artists", United States Embassy, Panama City, Panama

2002   "American Artists", United States Embassy, Riga, Latvia
       "American Artists", United States Embassy, Tallinn, Estonia
       "Two Artists", Friesen Fine Art, Seattle, WA
       "Fifteenth Anniversary Exhibition", Galerie Timothy Tew, Atlanta, GA
       "Affordable Art Fair", Cheryl Pelavin Fine Arts, New York, NY
       "The Head Show", Galerie Timothy Tew, Atlanta, GA
       "Reactions", Exit Art, New York, NY
       "Toxic Landscape: Artists Look at the Environment", Bibliotéca Nacional José Martí,
          Havana, Cuba

SELECTED GROUP EXHIBITIONS, CONTINUED

2001   "Group Exhibition", Friesen Fine Art, Seattle, WA
        "Group Exhibition", Norton Gallery, Seattle, WA
        "World Trade Center Benefit Exhibition", Cheryl Pelavin Fine Arts, New York, NY
2000   "Group Exhibition", Friesen Fine Art, Sun Valley, ID
1999   "American Artists", United States Embassy, Lima, Peru
        "American Artists", United States Embassy, Reykjavik, Iceland
        "American Artists", United States Embassy, Bangkok, Thailand
        "Sitting Pretty", Met Life Windows, New York, NY
        "Birdsong", Laurie Seeman Gallery, Nyack, NY
1998   "Visual Dialogues: 15 Women Artists", Robert Kidd Gallery, Detroit, MI
        "Nature/Culture", The New York Arts Exchange Show, New York, NY
        "Four Artists", Lone Star Park Gallery, Dallas, TX
        "Group Exhibition", Tower Air, curated by Jeannie Greenberg, New York, NY
1997   "Sizzle", Jeffrey Coploff Gallery, New York, NY
        "Group Exhibition", Hillwood Museum, Chattanooga, TN
        "Art of Hearts", Nora Haime Gallery & the National Academy of Design, New York, NY
        "Group Exhibition", Hodges Taylor Gallery, Charlotte, NC
        "The National Horse Show", Robert Kidd Gallery, Detroit, MI
1996   "Partners in Printmaking: Works from Solo Impressions",
            National Museum of Women in the Arts, Washington, DC
        "Painting Exhibition", Hillwood Museum, Long Island University, NY
        "Three Photographers", June Kelly Gallery, New York, NY
        "American Artists", United States Embassy, Muscat, Oman
        "Recent Monotype Editions", Pelavin Editions, New York, NY
        "Group Exhibition", Robert L. Kidd Gallery, Detroit, MI
1995   "American Artists", United States Embassy, Amman, Jordan
        "Inaugural Exhibition", Michele Bigue Gallery, Fort Lauderdale, FL
1994   "American Artists", United States Embassy, Oslo, Norway
        "Group Exhibition", ES Painting Space, New York, NY
1993   "Animal Imagery", Champion Paper, curated by Janice Oresman, Hartfield, CT
1992   "34 Raumes", Documenta, Berlin, Germany
        "Printmaking from the Permanent Collection", Jane Voorhees Zimmerli Art Museum,
            Rutgers University, NJ
        "Works on Paper from Pelavin Editions", The Armory Show, New York, NY
1991   "Works on Paper", Champion Paper, Stanford, CT
1990   "Intaglio Printing in the 1980's", Jane Voorhees Zimmerli Art Museum,
            Rutgers University, New Brunswick, NJ
        "Women in Print", Traveling museum exhibition,
            National Museum of Women in the Arts, Washington, DC
        "Menagerie", General Electric Company Headquarters,
            Curated by MOMA Advisory Services, CT
1989   "Surface Printing in the 1980's", Jane Voorhees Zimmerli Art Museum, Rutgers University,
            New Brunswick, NJ
        "Creatures", Benson Gallery, Bridgehampton, NY

1988   "Three Sculptors Working in Bronze", Gallerie Helene Grubair, Miami, FL
1987   "Group Show", Albright Knox Museum, Buffalo, NY
1986   "Monotypes by Gallery Artists", Oscarsson-Siegeltuch Gallery, New York, NY
        "Paintings", van Straaten Gallery, Chicago, IL
        "Inaugural Exhibition", Group Show, Oscarsson-Siegeltuch Gallery, New York, NY
        "Homage to Ana Mendieta", Zeus Trabia Gallery, New York, NY
        "Monotypes", Jay Gallery, New York, NY
1985   "Art of the 70's & 80's", Aldrich Museum of Contemporary Art, Ridgefield, CT
        "1985 Invitational Quinquennial Exhibition", Oscarsson Hood Gallery, New York, NY
        "Selections from the Jane Voorhees Zimmerli Art Museum", The Grolier Club, New York, NY
        "Chicago Art Expo", Oscarsson Hood Gallery, Chicago, IL
        "Pelavin Editions 1985", Jay Gallery, New York, NY
        "Monotypes and Works on Paper", Robert L. Kidd Gallery, Detroit, MI
        "Animals: Contemporary Visions", Robert L. Kidd Gallery, Detroit, MI
        "The Animal Within", Jay Gallery, New York, NY
        "Young Printmakers", Roger Ramsey Gallery, Chicago, IL
        "Two Artists", Peri Renneth Gallery, West Hampton, NY
1984   "Painting Invitational", Robeson Center Gallery, Rutgers University, New Brunswick, NJ
        "Situations", Jamaica Arts Center, The Newark Museum Collection, Newark, NJ
        "Review/Preview", Oscarsson Hood Gallery, New York, NY
        "Works on Paper", Wolff Gallery, New York, NY
        "8 at 84", Robert Feldman Gallery, New York, NY
        "Works on Paper", Barbara Greene Gallery, Miami, FL
        "Ringing in the New", Jay Gallery, New York, NY
1983   "New Acquisitions", Newark Museum, Newark, NJ
        "Art on Paper", Weatherspoon Museum, Greensboro, NC
        "Group Exhibition", Oscarsson Hood Gallery, New York, NY
        "Works on Paper", Frumpkin Struve Gallery, Chicago, IL
        "Group Show", Albright Knox Museum, Buffalo, NY
1982   "Group Show", Albright Knox Museum, Buffalo, NY
        "New Acquisitions", Alternative Museum, New York, NY
        "Mixed Bag", Alternative Museum, New York, NY
        "Group Exhibition", McNay Art Institute, Collectors Gallery VI, Austin, TX
        "Works on Paper", Roger Ramsey Gallery, Chicago, IL
        "Group Exhibition", Oscarsson Hood Gallery, New York, NY
1981   "New Acquisitions", Aldrich Museum of Contemporary Art, CT
        "Nine Artists Invited", Meisal Gallery, New York, NY
        "Group Exhibition", Semaphore Gallery, New York, NY
        "The Working Process", O.I.A. Exhibition, New York, NY
        "Group Exhibition", Newcomber Westreich Gallery, Washington, DC
1980   "Small Works", 80 Gallery, Washington Square East, New York, NY
        "Group Show," Race Gallery, Philadelphia, PA
        "4 Artists", Soho Center for Visual Artists, New York, NY
        "Betty Parsons at Robert L. Kidd Gallery", Robert L. Kidd Gallery, Detroit, MI

COLLECTIONS

MUSEUM COLLECTIONS
Alternative Museum, New York, NY
Herbert F. Johnson Museum, Cornell University, Ithaca, NY
National Museum of Women in the Arts, Washington, DC
Newark Museum, Newark, NJ
Orlando Museum of Art, Orlando, FL
Seattle Art Museum, Seattle, WA
Jane Voorhees Zimmerli Art Museum, Rutgers, NJ
Xianghai Museum, Xianghai Nature Reserve, Xianghai, China

SELECTED PUBLIC COLLECTIONS
Agrace Hospice Care, Madison, WI
Architectural Arts, Inc, Dallas, TX
Banca della Suizzeria Italiana, New York, NY
Bank Boston, Boston, MA
Barron & Budd, New York, NY
Chase Manhattan Bank, New York, NY
Chemical Bank, New York, NY
Citibank International, Miami, FL
Denrich Leasing Company, Miami, FL
Echo Lab, MN
Carey Ellis Company, MN
Ernst & Young, New York, NY
Evergreen Asset & Management Corporation, New York, NY
Federal Reserve Bank, Chicago, IL
First National Bank, Boston, MA
Fuzhou International Center, Fuzhou, China
General Instruments, New York, NY
General Mills, Inc, Minneapolis, MN
Goldman-Sachs, New York, NY
Gruntal, New York, NY
Henson & Effron, St. Paul, MN
Hospital Corporation of North America, Nashville, TN
IBM Collection, Los Angeles, CA
Indiana National Bank, Boston, TX
International Data Group, Boston, MA
Kempner Insurance Company, New York, NY
King Investment Advisor, Inc, Houston, TX
Lang Communications, New York, NY
Library of Congress (Exit Art Reactions Exhibition), Washington, DC
Sidney Lewis Collection, Richmond, VA
Martin Margulies Collection, Miami, FL

SELECTED PUBLIC COLLECTIONS, CONTINUED

Mayo Clinic, Rochester, MN
McDonalds Corporation, Oak Brook, IL
The Mercer Company, New York, NY
J. P. Morgan and Company, New York, NY
Morgan Guarantee, New York, NY
Nutter, McClennan and Fish, Boston, TX
Palm Hills Hotel, Okinawa, Japan
Peat, Marwich, Mitchell and Co, Montvale, NJ
Pew Charitable Trust, Philadelphia, PA
Pfizer Pharmaceuticals, Inc, New York, NY
Polsinelli Collection, Los Angeles, CA
Prudential Life Insurance Company, Rockefeller Center, New York, NY
Quad Graphics, West Allis, IL
Quaker Oats, Chicago, IL
Randolph & Tate Associates, New York, NY
Reich & Tang, New York, NY
Simpson, Thacher, Bartlett, New York, NY
Skadden, Arps, Slate, Meagher & Flom, New York, NY
Solomon Equities, Inc, New York, NY
Tower Air, New York, NY
United States Department of State, Washington, DC
Vinson Elkins, Houston, TX
Wachovia, Charlotte, NC
E.M. Warburg Pincus, New York, NY
WFAE National Public Radio, Charlotte, NC
C. Wright Design, Mill Valley, CA
Zale Corporation, Dallas, TX
Zelle & Larson, St. Paul, MN

INDIVIDUAL ARTIST GRANTS

2016   Fulbright Senior Specialist, India
2006   Pang Mapha Highland Archaeology Project, Visiting Artist Grant, Thailand
2003   Teaneck Creek Conservancy, Atlantic Flyway art installation, Teaneck, NJ
2002   Art in Embassies Program, US Department of State,
            Art Ambassador to the Baltics, Riga, Latvia
        Art in Embassies Program, US Department of State,
            Art Ambassador to the Baltics, Tallinn, Estonia
        The Puffin Foundation, paintings and photographs
2001   United States Embassy Grant, Visiting Artist, Bangkok, Thailand
1999   Pollock Krasner Foundation
1986   Pollock Krasner Foundation
1984   Ariana Foundation for the Arts
1983   Mid Atlantic States Consortium

REVIEWS | ONE-PERSON EXHIBITIONS

2006   THE NEW YORKER   17 April, 2006
Review by Martha Schwendener
One-person exhibition at Cheryl Pelavin Fine Arts, New York, NY

2005   THE WASHINGTON DIPLOMAT   "Larger Than Life: DuBasky's Oversize Work
Focuses on Animal, Plant Life Along Silk Road"   October, 2005
Review by Venessa LaFaso
One-person exhibition at the National Academy of Sciences Gallery, Washington, DC
Color reproductions: *Gray Bird and Branches,* 2005, *Riverbirds, Fossils and Reeds,* 2005,
and *Mountain Site,* 2003

     THE EXAMINER   29 October, 2005
Review by Robin Tierney
One-person exhibition at National Academy of Sciences Gallery, Washington, DC
Color Reproduction: *Red Bird and Reeds,* 2005

2001   TRIBECA TRIBUNE   Vol. 8, No. 4   December, 2001
Review by Jeanne C. Wilkinson
One-person exhibition at Cheryl Pelavin Fine Arts, New York, NY
Color Reproduction: *Forest Site Wat Phimai,* 2001

2000   THE NEW YORK TIMES   4 February, 2000
Review by Ken Johnson
One-person exhibition at Cheryl Pelavin Fine Arts, New York, NY

     REVIEW   January, 2000
Review by Joel Silverstein
One-person exhibition at Cheryl Pelavin Fine Arts, New York, NY

     IDAHO MOUNTAIN EXPRESS, ARTS & EVENTS, pC-2   2 August, 2000
Anon.
One-person exhibition at Andria Friesen Fine Arts, Seattle, WA
Color Reproduction: *Forest Site with Spotted Stag,* 2000

1999   ART IN AMERICA   January, 1999
Review by Gerrit Henry
One-person exhibition at Cheryl Pelavin Fine Arts, New York, NY
Color Reproduction: *Syntax,* 1998

1997   CHARLOTTE NEWSSTAND, ARTS & ENTERTAINMENT   1 November, 1997
Review by Jane Grau
One-person exhibition at Hodges Taylor Gallery, Charlotte, NC
Color Reproduction: *Red Spotted Horse,* 1997

1991   ARTFORUM   December, 1991
Review by Ronny Cohen
One-person exhibition at Ruth Siegel Gallery, New York, NY
Color Reproduction: *Indonesia,* 1991

1986   ART IN AMERICA   April, 1986
Review by Gerrit Henry
One-person exhibition at Oscarsson-Hood Gallery, New York, NY
Reproduction: *Primate,* 1986

THE WEEKLY   "Modern Day Cave Painting"   Vol. 11, No. 25   18 June, 1986
Review by Doen Broelley
One-person exhibition at Hodges Banks Gallery, Seattle, WA
Color Reproduction: *Sienna Stag,* 1984

1985   GALLERY GUIDE   December, 1985
Anon.
One-person exhibition at Oscarsson-Hood Gallery, New York, NY
Reproduction: *Rough Beast,* 1984

MIAMI NEWS, MIAMI ART SCENE   April, 1985
Review by Paula Harper
One-person exhibition at Gloria Luria Gallery, Miami, FL

WOMEN ARTISTS NEWS   "Prehistory to Post Modernism" Vol. 9, No. 2   Winter, 1983-4
Review by John Arthur Shanks
One-person exhibition at Oscarsson-Hood Gallery, New York, NY
Reproduction: *Fallow Deer in Bracken,* 1983

1983   ARTS MAGAZINE   1983
Review by William Zimmer
One-person exhibition at Oscarsson-Hood Gallery, New York, NY
Reproduction: *Amber Stag,* 1983

1981   ARTS MAGAZINE   Vol. 55, No. 6   1981
Review by Addison Parks
One-person exhibition at Semaphore Gallery, New York, NY
Color Reproduction: *Split Cow,* 1981

ARTSPEAK   Vol. 2, No. 9   1981
Review by William Pellicone
One-person exhibition at Semaphore Gallery, New York, NY
Reproduction: *Split Cow,* 1981

WOMEN ARTISTS NEWS   Winter/Spring, 1981
Review by John Arthur Shanks
One-person exhibition at Semaphore Gallery, New York, NY
Color Reproduction: *Split Cow,* 1981

ONLINE REVIEWS | ONE-PERSON EXHIBITIONS

2008   ABSOLUTEARTS.COM: INDEPTH ART NEWS   "Mongolian Horses and Siberian Tigers-New Paintings on Paper and Canvas"   23 October, 2008
One-person exhibition at Cheryl Pelavin Fine Arts, New York, NY
Color Reproduction: *Crouching Tiger,* 2008

REVIEWS | FEATURE ARTICLES

2006   THE NEW YORK SUN, ON THE TOWN   "Rain Clouds: Valentina DuBasky at Cheryl Pelavin Fine Arts"   18 May, 2006, p12
Anon.
Color Reproduction: *Riverbank Late Afternoon,* 2006

2003   ART & ANTIQUES   "Reimagining the Landscape: Contemporary Painters Bring Fresh Ideas and Techniques to a Classic Art Form"   Vol. 26, No. 10   October, 2003, p 71
Article by Edward M. Gomez
Color Reproduction: *Open Forest,* 2001

         MAKSLA PLUS, KULTURAS ZURNALS   "Amerikas maksla Riga"   Vol. 1, No. 33, February/ March, 2003, pgs 11 & 13
Article by Gundega Cebere
Color Reproduction: *Heron,* 1995 and *Heron, Warbler and Milkweed,* 1991

         STATE MAGAZINE   "The Art of Visual Diplomacy"   No. 464   January, 2003, pgs 1 and 13
Article by Elizabeth Ash

2002   ARCHITECTURE AND DESIGN IN THE BALTICS   "Old Birds Under One Roof"   No. 5 October, 2002, pgs 11 and 25
Article by Irina Osadchaja
Color reproductions: *Heron,* 1995 and *Heron, Warbler and Milkweed,* 1991

2000   SEATTLE WOOD RIVER JOURNAL   "Western Explorers Meet Explorations on Canvas and Film"   2 August, 2000, p1
Article by Susan Bailey
Color Reproduction: *Forest Site with River & Orchids,* 2000

         SUN VALLEY ART   "Painting/ Profile: Modern Landscape Painting"   Vol. 6, Nos. 8 & 9 February-March, 2000
Article by Meagan Stasz
Color reproductions: *Forest Site with Orchids & Wild Grass,* 2000 and
Forest Canopy & Botanicas, 2000

1986   ARTS MAGAZINE   "Hudson River Editions, Pelavin Editions-A Report Back from the Other World of Printmaking"   November, 1986, p42
Article by Timothy Cohrs
Color Reproduction: *Stag/Red Meander,* 1985

1981   THE WASHINGTON POST "Seventh Street Galleries Celebrate Reopening"
19 September 1981
Article by Joseph Mclellan

REVIEWS | TELEVISION FEATURES

WETA PUBLIC TELEVISION `AROUND TOWN/ BEST BETS WITH JANICE GOODMAN
5 August, 2005
Review by Janice Goodman
One-person exhibition of "Riverbirds & Rainforests" at the National Academy of Sciences Gallery, Washington, DC

APSARA TELEVISION   9 June, 2007
Cambodian Journal: One-person exhibition at the Java Arts, Phnom Penh, Cambodia

TELEVISION OF THAILAND CHANNEL   11 July, 2001
One-person exhibition, Silpakorn Gallery, Silpakorn University, Bangkok, Thailand

REVIEWS | PRINT PUBLICATIONS

2014   ART IN PRINT   "Selected New Editions"   March-April, 2014
Anon.
Color Reproduction: *Cliff Site with Red Heron,* monoprint, 2013

JOURNAL OF THE PRINT WORLD   "New Editions"   April/May/June, 2014
Anon.
Color Reproduction: *Amber Birds with Indigo Mountain,* monoprint, 2013

2001   IN NEW YORK/ ECLECTIC COLLECTOR   July, 2008
Review by Erin Szeto-Chan
Color Reproduction: *Tiger Orchid/ Sri Lanka,* monoprint, 2001

1992   TWENTY-FIRST CENTURY PRINTS   August, 1992
Review by Meri Marimo
Color Reproduction: *River Edge,* monoprint, 1990

1988   PRINT NEWS: INTERNATIONAL JOURNAL OF CONTEMPORARY PRINTS   Vol. 8, No. 2, 1988
Anon.
Color Reproduction: *Ragtime Hart,* monoprint,1985

1986   WEST SIDE SPIRIT/ ARTS & ENTERTAINMENT   "Ancient Art Comes Alive"   14 July, 1986
Review by Tom Beller
Color Reproductions: *Leaping Brindled Stag,* color etching, 1984, and
Ragtime Hart, monoprint, 1984

1984   ARTNEWS   "New Editions"   April, 1984
Review by Ronny Cohen
Color Reproduction: *Dune Horse/Starry Night,* lithograph, 1983

THE PRINT COLLECTORS NEWSLETTER   Vol. 15, No. 3   July-August, 1984
Anon.
Color Reproductions: *Claret Stag in Plum Field,* 1984; *Leaping Brindled Stag,* color etchings, 1984

1983   THE PRINT COLLECTORS NEWSLETTER   Vol. 14, No. 5
Anon.
Color Reproduction: *Dune Horse/Starry Night,* lithograph, 1983

REVIEWS | GROUP EXHIBITIONS

2000   TRIBUNE/REVIEW   "Pair of Shows Comment on Environmental Issues Facing Our Nation
and the World"   16 November, 2001
Review by Kurt Shaw

1988   THE MIAMI NEWS   "Sculpture is the focus of Gallery Show"   3 June, 1988
Review by Leslie Judd Ahlander
Reproduction: *Standing Camel,* 1988

1985   ARTNEWS   "Group Show: Wolff Gallery"   January, 1985
Review by Sarah Cecil

1983   DETROIT FREE PRESS   November, 1983
Review by Marsha Miro
Detroit News, November, 1983

1981   WHERE MAGAZINE   August, 1981
Anon.

1980   THE VILLAGE VOICE   "Reports from the Front"   Vol. 25, No. 7, 1980
Review by Kay Larsen

THE VILLAGE VOICE   1980
Review by Carrie Rickey

REVIEWS | INTERNATIONAL EXHIBITIONS

2007   THE CAMBODIA DAILY   "Back to Basics: Two Artists' Return to Drawing"   June, 2007
Review by Michelle Vachon
Color reproductions: *Crossing the Street in Hanoi,* 1994 and *Resting Soldier,* 1994

ASIA LIFE   "Cambodian Journal: Human resilience and the strong Cambodian spirit
are themes that artist Valentina DuBasky explores in her new exhibition"   2007
Review by Liz Ledden

2002   STATE MAGAZINE   "In the News: Artist and Their Art Go Abroad"   December, 2002, p5
Color Reproduction: *Heron, Warbler and Milkweed,* 1991

BANGKOK POST   "Ancient Futures: Cave-wall Landscape Paintings"   22 June 2001, p1
Color reproductions: *Forest Site with Orchids and Bending Trees,* 2000

2001   NAEW NA   "Ancient Futures: New Cave-Wall Landscape by Valentina DuBasky"   June, 2001

2000   THE NATION   "New and Old"   16 July, 2001
Color reproductions: *Forest Site with Orchids and Bending Trees,* 2000

SIAM RATH   "Ancient Futures"   21 June, 2001
Color reproductions: *Forest Site with Orchids and Bending Trees,* 2000, and
Forest Floor with Orchids, 2000

BANGKOK POST   "Ancient Futures: Cave-wall Landscape Paintings"   2000
Color Reproduction: *Forest Site with Stag and Bird,* 2000

2006   LUXE MAGAZINE, INTERIORS + DESIGN PACIFIC NORTHWEST EDITION   "Tall Order"
Issue 1, Vol. 8   Winter, 2010, p178
Article by Linda Hayes
Color Reproduction: *River Fragments Grey Bird,* 1990

THE LAKEVILLE JOURNAL   10 August, 2006, pC12
Reproduction: *Eurasian Steppe Horse,* 2004

2002   SOUTHERN VOICE Atlanta   11 October, 2002
Article by Christopher Seely
Color Reproduction: *Yellow Bird in Grey Field,* 2002

2000   IDAHO MOUNTAIN EXPRESS, ARTS & EVENTS SUN VALLEY   2 August, 2000
Color Reproduction: *Forest Site with Spotted Stag,* 2000

1999   THE SCIENCES MAGAZINE   Volume 39, No. 4, p5   July/August 1999
Color Reproduction: *Pond Site,* 1999

1997   CAROLINA ARTS   "Hodges Taylor Gallery is Moving"   Vol. 1, No. 9   1997, p19
Color Reproduction: *Red Spotted Horse,* 1997

SOUTHERN ACCENTS Charlotte   1997
Color Reproduction: *Red Horse/ Split,* 1997

1992   CHRISTIAN SCIENCE MONITOR   23 November, 1992
Color Reproduction: *Heron Cove,* 1990

1991   THE MENNIGER PERSPECTIVE   Issue No. 3, 1991
Color Reproduction: *Eastern Quarter,* 1991

1990   MS MAGAZINE poster publication
Color Reproduction: *Heron Cove,* 1990

1988   THE POLLOCK KRASNER FOUNDATION ANNUAL REPORT   1987-1988
Reproduction: *Strata,* 1984

LEGACY FOUNDATION
Color cover Reproduction: *Good Medicine,* 1996

1985   THE SCIENCES MAGAZINE   "The Ancestor that Wasn't"   March/April, 1985, p46
Color Reproduction: *Back to Back,* 1984

1983   THE NEWARK MUSEUM ANNUAL REPORT
Reproduction: *Bucks Country,* 1983

1980   MAENAD MAGAZINE
Color cover Reproduction: *Spotted Bison,* and 4 paintings, 1980

EXHIBITION CATALOGS

2016   THE JOURNEY OF THE RED HORSE: HORSE AND STAG PAINTINGS
by Valentina DuBasky
Published by Abingdon Square Publishing
Color reproductions: 13 color plates

2015   KINETIV: HIGHLIGHTS FROM THE POLSINELLI ART COLLECTION, image: pg 94
Edited by Mary Walsh
Published by Polsinelli
Color reproduction: *Amber Birds with Indigo Mountain,* 2013

2008   FROM [DIFFERENT] HORIZONS OF ROCKSHELTER
Exhibition catalog essay by Rasmi Shoocongdej
Published by Silpakorn University Press, Bangkok, Thailand
Color reproductions: 6 paintings from the Pang Mapha Highland Archaeology Project

2005   RIVERBIRDS AND RAINFOREST PAINTINGS BY VALENTINA DUBASKY AT
THE NATIONAL ACADEMIES OF SCIENCES
Exhibition catalog essay by Cynthia Nadelman; **Forward** by JD Talasek
Published by the National Academies of Sciences, Washington, DC
Color reproductions: 11 color plates

2003   UNITED STATES EMBASSY PANAMA: ARTS IN EMBASSY PROGRAM, images: pgs 6 and 7
Exhibition catalog essay by United States Ambassador Linda E. Watt
Printed by the United States Department of State
Color reproductions: *Untitled,* 1998, *Shore Site,* 1991 and *Rainforest,* 1999

2002   ART IN EMBASSIES EXHIBITION AT THE RESIDENCE OF THE AMERICAN AMBASSADOR
RIGA, LATVIA
Exhibition catalog essay by United States Ambassador Brian E. Carlson
Printed by the United States Department of State
Color reproductions: *Heron, Warbler and Milkweed,* 1991 (cover) and *Heron,* 1995

          TOXIC LANDSCAPES: ARTISTS EXAMINE THE ENVIRONMENT, image: p20
Printed by the Puffin Foundation
Reproduction: *Tragic Harvest,* 1991

2001   FORESTS, ORCHIDS & FOSSILS BY VALENTINA DUBASKY   7 November, 2001
Exhibition catalog essay by Gerrit Henry
Color reproductions: 9 color plates

1999   OIL & WAX: CHAPTER & VERSE
Color Reproduction: *Spotted Horse,* 1999

1998   AMERICAN ARTISTS AT AMERICAN AMBASSADOR'S RESIDENCES
MUSCAT, SULTANATE OF OMAN, images: p14
Exhibition catalog essay by United States Ambassador Frances D. Cook
Printed by United States Department of State
Color Reproduction: *Heron Cove,* 1990

EXHIBITION CATALOGS, CONTINUED

1990   PRESSWORK: THE ART OF WOMEN PRINTMAKERS
       Exhibition catalog essays by Eleanor Heartney and Trudy Hanson
       Printed by Lang Publications, 1990
       Color Reproduction: *Heron Cove,* 1990

1987   THE NEW YORK ART REVIEW
       Printed by the American References Publishing Corporation, Chicago, IL

1985   INTAGLIO PRINTING IN THE 1980'S
       Printed by the Jane Voorhees Zimmerli Art Museum

1984   RUTGERS ARCHIVES FOR PRINTMAKING STUDIOS, CATALOG OF ACQUISITIONS,
       1985-1987
       Printed by the Jane Voorhees Zimmerli Art Museum, Rutgers University
       Reproductions: *Red Stag Diptych,* 1984, *Leaping Brindled Stag,* 1984, *Claret Stag in Plum Field,* 1984, *Small Stag Series,* 1984, and *Gray Stag/ Ochre Field,* 1984

       SURFACE PRINTING IN THE 1980'S; LITHOGRAPHS, SCREENPRINTS & MONOPRINTS
       FROM THE RUTGERS ARCHIVES FOR PRINTMAKING STUDIOS
       Exhibition catalog essay by Donna Gustafon
       Printed by the Jane Voorhees Zimmerli Art Museum, Rutgers University
       Reproduction: *Gray Stag/Ochre Field,* 1984

1981   THE WORKING PROCESS
       Color Reproduction: *Untitled,* 1981

       MIXED BAG, image, p12
       Exhibition catalog essay by Robert Browning
       Printed by the Alternative Museum
       Reproduction: *Cumulus on the Mount,* 1981

COVERS

2005   THE NATIONAL ACADEMIES PRESS TRADE OFFERINGS
       Published by Joseph Henry Press
       Color Reproduction: *Cranes, Warblers and Ironwood,* 2003

2005   THE NATIONAL ACADEMIES PRESS NEW AND FORTHCOMING BOOKS
       Published by Joseph Henry Press
       Color Reproduction: *Shore Site,* 2005

1996   LEGACY FOUNDATION
       Color Reproduction: *Good Medicine,* 1996

FINE ART PRINT PUBLICATIONS

2013   TANDEM PRESS
Large scale monoprints and lithograph publication

1984-2008 PELAVIN EDITIONS, LTD
Large scale monoprints and etching publication

1983   SOLO PRESS
Mixed media lithograph

BOOK PUBLICATIONS

2016   A SILK ROUTE BESTIARY: PAINTINGS AND TEXT
by Valentina DuBasky
Published by Abingdon Square Publishing (forthcoming)
Color reproductions: 60 color plates

2011   NICHOLAS NEVIUS
by Lee Barnes, illustrations by Valentina DuBasky
Published by Abingdon Square Publishing
Color reproductions: 25 color plates

2009   THE CAMBODIAN JOURNAL: DRAWINGS 1994-1998
by Valentina DuBasky
Published by Abingdon Square Publishing
Color reproductions: 35 color plates

2002   SOUL SURVIVORS: STORIES OF WOMEN & CHILDREN IN CAMBODIA
by Carol Bhavia Wagner, photographs by Valentina DuBasky
Published by Wild Iris Press
Reproductions: 64 photographs

LIST OF PLATES

www.ingramcontent.com/pod-product-compliance
Lightning Source LLC
Chambersburg PA
CBHW050439180526
45159CB00006B/2601